Iveagh House

Written by
Nicholas Sheaff.

Iveagh House

An historical description

Published by
Department of Foreign Affairs, Dublin, Ireland.

Dublin 1978.

*Nicholas Sheaff was born
in Liverpool in 1953. He
was educated at the King's
School, Chester, and at
Clare College, Cambridge.
He began work in Ireland in
1976, as a research
assistant on the
forthcoming Penguin Books
series,* The Buildings of
Ireland, *and later the same
year was appointed
Director of the National
Trust Archive, Dublin. He is
a member of An Taisce, the
Irish Georgian Society and
the Dublin Civic Group.*

ISBN 0 906404 02 9

Design by Bill Murphy, MSIA.
Printed by Mount Salus Press Ltd.

Contents

7 **Acknowledgements**

9 **Introduction**

11 **The eighteenth-century house**
The setting: St Stephen's Green – The patron: Bishop Clayton –
The architect: Richard Castle — Later owners

19 **The nineteenth-century house**
The Guinness family – The creation of the modern Iveagh House –
The remodelling of St Stephen's Green

25 **Iveagh House in the present century**

27 **Description of the house**
the exterior – the entrance hall – the inner hall —
the old dining-room — the ante-room - the stairhall –
the old music-room — the saloon — the front drawing-room
the drawing-room — the old library –– the ballroom vestibule
the Adam room — the ballroom

55 **Iveagh Gardens**

57 **Appendix**

59 **List of plates with acknowledgements**

61 **References**

63 **Index**

Acknowledgements

My thanks for help received in writing this short study are due first to the board of directors of the National Trust Archive, Dublin, who have kindly allowed time for research during office hours when my historical investigations required it. In particular I have pleasure in thanking two of the directors, Dr Edward McParland and Desmond Fitz-Gerald, Knight of Glin, for their keen interest in the project and for their valuable comments on the typescript.

For their generous assistance on specific points, I should like to thank the following: Mr Martin Burke, Professor Anne Crookshank, Mr Bertie Foy, Mr David Griffin, Professor Matthew McDermott, Mr Rory O'Donnell and Mrs Lesley Whiteside. My special thanks are due to Miss Siobhán Murphy who typed the manuscript; and to Mr James Bambury, Senior Photographer at the Office of Public Works, Dublin, whose patience and skill are reflected in the illustrations to the text.

Lastly and equally my thanks go to the staff of the following institutions for the assistance they have given to my work: the National Library of Ireland, the Public Record Office, Dublin, the Registry of Deeds, Dublin, the Royal Irish Academy, and the library of Trinity College, Dublin.

Iveagh House

Introduction

Dublin abounds in hidden architectural splendours. Behind the reticent façades of the city's great mansions there is to be found a remarkable series of decorative interiors which is unique to Ireland and is equalled in its variety by few other European capitals. Access to this sparkling and ostentatious world is generally limited to the curious and determined, but many observant passers-by will have been arrested in the early evening by a blaze of light indoors, revealing a monumental classical hall or the crisp foliage patterns of a rococo ceiling.

This element of surprise, one of the most compelling attractions of Dublin's historic houses, is embodied memorably in the architecture and decorations of Iveagh House. Though the importance of the building is indicated by a distinguished façade, the beauty and spectacle of its interior will astonish many.
As the building is not open to the public, it is hoped that the text and illustrations in the present booklet will convey to the general reader something of the character of this historic house.

Iveagh House is exceptional among Dublin mansions for the consistency of purpose which has governed its construction, enlargement and use. The building has always played a significant rôle in the life of the city and has been owned by a series of powerful and discriminating people. The architectural fabric which they have passed down to us reflects an unswerving pursuit of beauty and excellence, ranging from the Palladian rationalism of the 18th-century saloon to the 19th-century stairhall and ballroom, where the decorative finery characteristic of Dublin interiors is united with the swaggering pomp of late Victorian classicism.

The architectural history of the building, from its construction in 1736 up to the present, is one of constant alteration and enlargement. Indeed, it could be said that this is not the description of one but of two houses, the first dating from 1736, the second from 1866, with frequent additional alterations along the way. In a house of this age and significance, it is important to understand the process of maintenance and alteration which has shaped it and, where the following description indulges in the dissection of parts of the house into features dating from different periods, it is my hope that the text will not read like notes taken at an anatomy lesson. It is the object of the description to analyse the personality of Iveagh House as we experience it today, as a culmination of the creative work of owners and architects over more than two centuries.

The modern use of Iveagh House gives contemporary relevance to an historic tradition. Since its presentation to the Irish nation by the second Earl of Iveagh in 1939, it has been the headquarters of Ireland's Department of Foreign Affairs. The careful and unobtrusive adaptation of the building to serve the needs of a modern government department is an affirmation of one of the guiding principles of European Architectural Heritage Year, recorded in the Amsterdam Declaration of October 1975—that historic buildings can be given new functions related to the needs of contemporary life.

The eighteenth-century house

The setting: St Stephen's Green

The 18th-century town mansion of Bishop Clayton, which today is incorporated in Iveagh House, was constructed in 1736 on the south side of a square which had already been in existence for seventy-five years. The square, St Stephen's Green, was the first to be created in Dublin. At thirty (English) acres it was one of the largest in Europe, embodying in its layout an amplitude which was to govern the planning of Dublin for over a century.

In the 17th century, the city of Dublin burst out of its mediaeval confines and encompassed land previously on its outskirts. The conversion of St Stephen's Green from a marshy meadow into a tree-lined square was part of this process. Lots were drawn for the building land around its perimeter in 1664, and from the first the City Assembly envisaged building development of a high quality. It was stipulated that any lot-holders who wished to build "... *be engaged to build of brick, stone and timber, to be covered with tiles or slates, with at least two floores or loftes, and a cellar, if they please to digg it ....*"[1]

Improvements to the great meadow at the centre followed rapidly, paid for by the ground rents on the building sites. In 1669, the square was levelled, and a deep ditch dug around the sward to drain it. On either side of the ditch were walks, the inner of grass lined with hawthorn hedges, the outer of gravel lined with lime trees and with a low stone wall to separate it from the street. Before long, the square became a fashionable place of promenade; "... *why don't you walk in the Green of St Stephen?*" Swift wrote to Stella and Mrs Dingley in 1710.[2] "... *the walks there are finer gravelled than the Mall.*" In 1731, the noted letter-writer Mrs Mary Pendarves (later Mrs Delany) visited St Stephen's Green, and considered it preferable to any square she had seen in London. Yet Brooking's map of 1728 shows that the square was actually incomplete at this time, and it remained so until the late 1740s. Only gradually did the sides of St Stephen's Green acquire the saw-tooth outlines which distinguish it from Dublin's later, more rationally planned squares, and which it owes to its irregular 17th-century building plots.

There was no more tendency towards uniformity in the architecture which rose on the plots than in the plots themselves. Bishop Clayton's house established a high architectural standard, both in its façade and interior fittings, which was followed by a dozen or so other private dwellings on St Stephen's Green over the next half-century, three of them—Nos. 85, 119 and 120—designed by the architect of Clayton's house, Richard Castle. But a uniformly high quality was never achieved—to the disgust of Malton, who railed both at the "... *indifferent old brick dwellings* ..." of the 1720s and "... *the modern plain taste of building* ..." of the 1790s.[3]

The completion of the sides of the square spurred on the improvement of the central common. In 1746, the limes were replanted, and in 1749 the square received a temporary embellishment in the form of a 'dodecagon' Temple of Peace, the gilded focus of a firework show in celebration of the peace concluded at Aix-la-Chapelle.[4] Enclosed by a balustrade of lighted obelisks, pillars and rockets, this was Dublin's own version of the festival architecture of Rome. In 1756, a more conventional centrepiece for St Stephen's Green was installed, Van Nost's brass equestrian statue of George II, on a massive limestone podium, emblazoned with military trophies and the letters *SPQD*, (Senatus Populusque Dubliniensis).

This, therefore, was the historical background to that *'resort of beauty and gaiety'*[5] depicted by Malton. But there were challenges to order and elegance. The brass monarch was frequently set upon at night by rowdies with hacksaws, whose interests were monetary rather than aesthetic. And due to an inadequate drainage system, the Green was returned in winter to its former swampiness, attracting flocks of wild birds and, in their turn, eager huntsmen. In 1752, the Lord Mayor, fearful of the danger to passers-by, introduced a bye-law forbidding the shooting of snipe there,[6] with the result that St Stephen's Green became a sanctuary for wildfowl—as the Dublin historian Walter Harris[7] noted "... *an agreeable and most uncommon circumstance, not to be met with, perhaps, in any other great city in the world.*"

2

The patron: Bishop Clayton

Dr Robert Clayton, the 18th-century Bishop whose town house forms the core of the modern Iveagh House, was, for a variety of reasons, one of the outstanding figures of Ireland in his day. He was a suave personality, a leading churchman but also a noted arbiter of taste, well-known for his pursuit of antiquarian and philosophical interests. One writer[1] characterized him skilfully as *'uniting the dignity of the ecclesiastic with the ease of the fine gentleman'*. That such a man should have ended his career in disgrace gives a tragic and unexpected twist to his lifestory.

Clayton was born in 1695, into a wealthy family with large estates at Fulwood in Lancashire. His father, Rev. John Clayton, became Dean of Kildare, and had a reputation as both an orator and intriguer. Robert's outstanding intellect revealed itself at an early age. He entered Trinity College, Dublin, distinguished himself in the Classics, and in 1714 became one of the youngest Fellows in the history of the College. Trinity remained the focus of Clayton's energies until the death of his father in 1725, when, coming into a large inheritance, he decided to abandon the celibate life of a don.

Clayton resigned his Fellowship and married Catherine Donnellan in June 1728. She was the daughter of a former Lord Chief Justice of the Exchequer in Ireland and a woman who was her husband's equal in both intelligence and energy. Though their marriage proved childless, they were to remain devoted. Shortly after their wedding, they probably embarked for Italy on the Grand Tour, a cultural expedition newly fashionable for those with the wealth to indulge educated tastes.

In 1729, the Claytons returned to London, accompanied by paintings, statuary and books — the spoils of their travels. Robert Clayton now turned his attention to a career in the Protestant church in Ireland, for which his academic studies had ideally prepared him.

The way that Clayton set about establishing himself as a prominent churchman reveals that he was prepared to go to great lengths in pursuit of power and influence. He had at court a relation, a former favourite of the Duchess of Marlborough, who had risen in court circles to become the confidante and mentor of Queen Caroline. This was Mrs Clayton, Mistress of the Robes, who was created Viscountess Sundon of Ardagh in 1735. Her influence over the Queen was resented by many, including the chief minister, Robert Walpole.[2]

It is clear that during his stay in London, Robert Clayton cultivated Mrs Clayton's patronage, thereby gaining favour at Court. He seems also to have been influenced permanently by the religious position of Mrs Clayton's circle, which was strongly low church in character and followed the teachings of Dr Samuel Clarke, Rector of St James's, Westminster. Clarke had declared his opposition to the doctrine of the Trinity in various writings, and Clayton adopted a similar theological position in later years.

Clayton succeeded in winning royal favour and in May 1730, was consecrated Bishop of Killala. Though busy with introductions to Dublin's influential circles, he found time to write in obsequious tones to his patroness: *"Since my arrival, my time has been entirely taken up in receiving and paying of visits. I went to pay my compliments to the Lords Justices . . . . The rest of the nobility of this city have been all to see me. They are not ignorant of the favours which Mrs Clayton was pleased to show me at London."*[3]

Mrs Pendarves, a friend from London, visited the Bishop and his wife in September 1731. Their house *". . . which indeed is magnifique . . ."*[4], as Mrs Pendarves commented, was on St Stephen's Green, but not on the site of today's Iveagh House. It was an earlier residence, probably on the west side of the square, near York Street.[5] Mrs Pendarves compared its façade to Devonshire House in London, a red brick and stone mansion of 1664 by Hugh May.

Mrs Pendarves stayed with the Claytons through the Dublin season and, in May 1732, was persuaded to join their expedition to the Bishop's Palace in Killala.

Her amused reaction[6] to Killala Cathedral, a western outpost of low church Protestantism, is worth repeating here: *"Perhaps you would think our cathedral a vulgar one, and that we have an organ and choir; no! we have no such popish doings—a good parish minister and bawling of psalms is our method of proceeding! The church is neat, but you would not dream it was a cathedral!"* Her host, on the other hand, won her admiration :*". . . one of the best of men, so even-tempered and obliging, everybody is at liberty to do what they like, and he is never so well pleased as when his company is diverted".*[7]

The Bishop tired rapidly of Killala and, through the influence of his powerful kinswoman, he was translated in 1735 to the Bishopric of Cork and Ross. Lord Orrery's account of him[8] dates from this time: *"We are not entirely void of Elegance at Corke. We have a Bishop, who, as He has travel'd beyond the Alps, has brought home with him . . . the Arts and Sciences that are the Ornament of Italy and the Admiration of the European World. He eats, drinks, and sleeps in Taste. He has pictures by Carlo Morat, Music by Corelli, Castles in the Air by Vitruvius, and on High-Days and Holidays We have the honour of catching Cold at a Venetian door.*[9] *To crown All, he is nearly allied to Lady Sundon . . . "*

The promotion to Cork prompted the Claytons, in 1736, to build themselves a new town house and this building today forms the 18th-century core of Iveagh House. It was designed in the newly-fashionable Italian manner by Richard Castle, the leading architect of the day. Lord Orrery visited the site during construction and was impressed: *"Your palace, my Lord, appears finely upon Paper, and to shew You that the whole pleases me, I even admire your Coal Cellars."*[10] But Mrs Pendarves, whose tastes were less ostentatious, considered the house *". . . very magnificent but more for show than comfortable living."*[11]

It was probably in the mid-1730s, prompted by his success, that the Bishop commissioned a double portrait of himself and his wife, painted by James Latham (plate 2). It skilfully captures their energy as well as their mutual affection. The Bishop turns from his studies towards his wife, whose bearing is tenser, her eyes sharp and penetrating.

In 1745, Dr Clayton was appointed Bishop of Clogher. It is clear that middle age had only confirmed the Claytons' grandiloquent tastes. Besides their Dublin house, there was the *"showish"*[12] Bishop's palace at Clogher and in 1752 they bought a country villa in Co. Kildare, St Woolstan's.[13] Mrs Delany—the former Mrs Pendarves, now remarried and settled in Dublin—found herself increasingly out of sympathy with their behaviour; *". . . they are so much engaged in the hurry and grandeur of the world, that they have not now any time to enjoy the more rational pleasures of friendship and conversation."* [14] The decline in their once cordial relations with Mrs Delany is reflected in the witty epithets she adopted for them in the 1750s—*"the Cardinal"* and *"Cardinella".*

With advancing years, the Bishop returned to the scholarly interests of his earlier years and, ironically enough, it was these which led to the ruination of his career. In 1751, he published anonymously a book entitled *An Essay on Spirit*[15] with the object of proving that the doctrine of the Trinity needed reform, something of which he had been convinced since his days in London. The book had a long preface which attempted to counter the charge that the *Essay* was heretical. But, notwithstanding this, the book aroused strong controversy and there was sufficient suspicion over its authorship for Clayton to be passed over for the promotion he had expected to the Archbishopric of Tuam. Further prolix works followed, on subjects theological, philosophical and bibliological. In 1753, there was a *Defence of the Essay on Spirit* and a work on hieroglyphics in Sinai; in 1754, a study of the philosophy of Hume and Bolingbroke and in 1755, a debate on the meaning of baptism, in letters to William Penn.[16]

In 1756, Clayton returned, fatally, to his favourite and most controversial themes, anti-Trinitarianism and reform of the Articles. His vehicle was a speech in the House of Lords in Dublin, which, taken down in

3. *Drawing of the marble chimney-piece on the ground-floor of the garden wing.*

shorthand and published,[17] linked his name unquestionably with *An Essay on Spirit*. Orders arrived from London for ecclesiastical proceedings to start against him and loss of his bishopric was certain. Clayton, betrayed by his intellectual ambitions and shunned by former friends, became deranged. He died at St Stephen's Green of a fever on 26 February 1758, aged sixty-four. His wife, who inherited a great fortune, died in 1766, and was buried alongside him.

Clayton's tombstone still survives in the old churchyard at Donnybrook, bearing a rather equivocal epitaph: *"His character as a Christian and abilities as a writer appear by his works."* A more evocative final word comes from Dr. Edward Barry,[18] the celebrated physician, who attended Clayton in his last illness: *"He was a good natur'd and polite man and often agreeable but He mistook his Talents as well as his subject. Want of Sleep probably made him an Author. A bad Poet gives the same reason to Horace who dissuades him from Verses—sed nequeo dormire."*

3

The architect: Richard Castle

The town house built by Bishop Clayton forms the core around which Iveagh House was built, and the 18th-century building still survives in its main internal elements. But as the plan on page 28 shows, it is boxed in to left and right by 19th-century additions, and is concealed behind a 19th-century façade.

Bishop Clayton's house was begun in the latter half of 1736, and was probably not completed until the spring of 1737. The site, lot fifteen on the south side of St Stephen's Green, was purchased in June 1736, for £250.[1] Payments for ground rent began in September, indicating that construction had started.[2] When Lord Orrery visited the site early in December, he found the walls standing but not yet roofed over.

The designer of the building was the German-born architect-engineer, Richard Castle (c. 1690-1751). Castle came to Ireland in 1728,[3] and began work immediately on the first of a series of country house commissions. He was also employed by Edward Lovett Pearce as his draughtsman and assistant on the new Parliament House which was rising on College Green. Pearce was one of the most brilliant and eclectic architects of the British Palladian school. Recognizing outstanding abilities in Castle, Pearce made him his protégé and was instrumental in promoting Castle's career. On Pearce's sudden death in 1733, Castle inherited a number of commissions and, by the mid-1730s, he had become the leading architect in Ireland.

Castle's reputation as an architect had been established by his country house commissions, frequently in remote parts of Ireland. From 1736, however, his career changed course, with a series of major works in Dublin which mark a watershed between his early country houses and those of the 1740s. Bishop Clayton's house was the first of this series and Castle's first commission for a town house.

The Clayton house provides us with an eye-witness account of Richard Castle, in a letter from Lord Orrery to Bishop Clayton, of December 1736. "*My Lord,—this comes to congratulate your Lord[p] upon your new House in Stevens-Green . . . Mr. Percival was so kind as to go with me there yesterday; and Signor Cassells [Castle] honoured us with his Company; but as your Lord[ps] Commands did not extend so far as to order me to break my Neck or my Limbs, I ventur'd no further than the Hall Door, from whence my Prospect was much confin'd, except when I look'd upwards to the sky. Your palace, my Lord, appears finely upon Paper . . . Your great Room will probably bring the Earl of Burlington[4] over to this Kingdom . . . however—I am in some Fear that your Smell will not be regal'd from your Stables . . . so that the Stable has a beautiful Cornish [cornice], Signor Cassells does not seem to care where it stands.*"[5]

Orrery's reference here to the cornice of a stable building emphasizes the careful attention to decorative detail which distinguishes all of Castle's best buildings. Indeed, it is known that he had the habit—like some Italian Renaissance architects—of pulling down work which did not achieve the precise effect he desired.[6] Castle's architecture is characterized by great accomplishment in working with a restricted number of compositional elements. Sensitive proportions and inventive detailing combine with these to produce a robust and masculine manner which distinguishes such works as Hazlewood, Co. Sligo, Ballyhaise, Co. Cavan, and Leinster House, Dublin. The house for Bishop Clayton also embodied the main qualities of Castle's classical style.

The façade of Bishop Clayton's house is reconstructed in plate 7.[7] It was three storeys high, with a basement, and three bays wide. It was surmounted by a hipped roof. To the left of the house, a carriageway led to the stables and coach-house at the rear, and to the right was a two-storeyed projection containing the end portions of rooms overlooking the garden. The basement and ground-floor were of cut stone, and above first-floor level the façade was of brick dressed with stone.

Castle, in typical manner, used no elaborate articulation of the façade, but chose rather the restrained interplay of a few carefully-modelled architectural features. The result was handsome and unaffected. The windows of the great saloon on the first floor were given emphasis, as befits the *piano nobile*, and the main cornice of the building was skilfully placed between the first and second floors, where it corresponded to the high cove of the saloon ceiling within.

The most interesting feature of the exterior was its four-columned entrance portico. This spread across the width of the façade, and was inspired by the portico designed by Inigo Jones for St Paul's Church, Covent Garden, London, a building admired by Castle.[8] While Castle used Jones's Tuscan order and square end piers, there was not enough room for a pediment, and so the portico was given a flat roof. This created problems later in the century, for the sheet lead of the roof fell victim to the St Stephen's Green scrap-metal thieves, on more than one occasion. About 1788,[9] an exasperated owner removed the portico, seemingly to the rear of the house, to the garden wing.

Bishop Clayton's house is a key building in the history of 18th-century domestic architecture in Dublin. Its façade, with the first projecting portico seen on a Dublin house, possessed a classical monumentality generally lacking in the brick Anglo-Dutch architecture of the previous half-century. Pearce had led the way towards this new monumentality with two houses in Henrietta Street, Dublin, Nos. 9 and 10, but there the façades had been designed as part of the street frontage. Richard Castle went further, designing Clayton's house to be free-standing, an aristocratic *palazzo* detached from its neighbours. Bishop Clayton's house embodied to the full the *grand gusto* of Palladianism, both in its internal arrangements and its façade, and was the first of several major Dublin town houses designed by Richard Castle in this style. It was followed by No. 85 St Stephen's Green; Bective House, Smithfield; Tyrone House, Marlborough Street; and Leinster House, the culmination of the genre.

Later owners

After the death of Bishop Clayton, his wife—who in accordance with his wishes[1] never remarried—continued to live in the house on St Stephen's Green. She died in 1766, and the house was purchased in June 1767[2] by Stephen, second Viscount Mountcashel, who became first Earl of Mountcashel in 1781. For forty years the house was known as 'Mountcashel House', and some significant alterations were made to the fabric during this period—the installation of ornamental plasterwork inside, probably soon after Mountcashel bought the house (see page 34), and the removal of the entrance portico, probably in 1788.
The first Earl died in 1790, and the Countess in 1792.

Stephen, second Earl of Mountcashel, only remained in the house a few years, selling it in 1807. In 1809, it was purchased by the Rt Hon. John Philpot Curran, for £3,000. Curran was one of the most celebrated wits of late 18th-century Dublin,[3] a parliamentarian and barrister, and a notable patriot. He acted as defending counsel for many of the United Irishmen. Curran's daughter, Sarah, was engaged to marry Robert Emmet, at the time of the rebellion led by him in 1803, and Curran's subsequent treatment of her was harsh and peremptory. She died in 1804. In 1806, he was appointed Master of the Rolls, but his later years were ones of bitterness and disillusion, and in 1814 he resigned the post. An auction of his household possessions was held at St Stephen's Green in the same year and in 1817 he died in London. Curran's tomb, surmounted by a splendid sarcophagus, is in the cemetery at Glasnevin.

In June 1814, Curran sold his house to his successor as Master of the Rolls, The Rt Hon. Sir William McMahon, for £3,400.[4] McMahon sold the house to another barrister, Charles Burton, in 1819, for £4,500.[5] Burton was appointed Justice of the King's Bench in 1820, and remained in the house until his death in 1847. Burton's son-in-law, a barrister named Robert Beatty West, owned the house for a few years, and after his death it passed to the Commissioners of Encumbered Estates—his estate, like many following the years of famine,

being overloaded with debts. It was purchased in
May 1856 from the Commissioners by Benjamin
Lee Guinness.[6] He bought it at a bargain price,
£2,500 and this sum was paid to the credit of the
estate of West's widow, Elisa.

4

4. Sir Benjamin Lee Guinness. Bronze statue by J H Foley erected in 1875 in the precincts of St Patrick's Cathedral, Dublin.

The Guinness family

When Benjamin Lee Guinness (1798-1868) bought the house built by Bishop Clayton, its rather sober early 19th-century mood was dispelled. He was the head of Ireland's greatest industrial concern, the brewery of Arthur Guinness, Son, and Company,[1] and following his purchase of the house, three generations of the Guinness family made it their Dublin home, adding to the grandeur of its fabric and reviving its reputation for splendid entertaining.

From 1840, Benjamin Lee was the controlling partner in the family business, but he had great regard for his father, Arthur Guinness, and was guided by his advice on most matters. His father died in 1855 and only then did Guinness start to play the prominent role in public life which his industrial achievements had justified. An outward sign of this was his decision, in 1856, to sell his family home in Thomas Street, alongside the brewery, and to move to St Stephen's Green.

Benjamin Lee Guinness was a man of strongly evangelical religious beliefs, and the central concerns of his life were his home and his work. Family life was warm and affectionate and, though it was set in opulent surroundings, was firmly disciplined. He regarded his wealth seriously, as a responsibility, believing it was his duty to use it for the public good. In this spirit, he was elected Conservative MP for Dublin in 1865 and, more particularly, acted as the sponsor of two great public works in Dublin in the last decade of his life. These were the restoration of St Patrick's Cathedral, and the Dublin Exhibition Palace project.

The first of these schemes, the restoration of St Patrick's Cathedral, was begun in 1860 and completed in 1863 at a cost to Guinness of over £110,000.[2] His munificent intervention to save the mediaeval cathedral from collapse was greeted with enthusiasm by the public and, in 1875, a statue of Guinness by J H Foley was erected in the precincts of St Patrick's as a testimonial (plate 4). The restoration had a symbolic significance for many Irish Protestants, as was revealed by an article in the *Daily Express* in 1865,[3] which called Guinness ". . . a

staunch defender of the Irish Church. The restorer of our National Cathedral is not the man to be found advocating or justifying, with Mr Gladstone, the destruction of the Establishment in this country."

The architectural profession was generally critical, however. Though the restoration had been started with the guidance of professional architects, Guinness himself rapidly took over the direction of operations and made some serious errors in judging which features merited preservation. J J McCarthy, Ireland's leading Gothic revival architect, was particularly vigilant and censorious.[4] But the restoration was undeniably sympathetic for its date, in that the character of the mediaeval building survived largely intact.

The second public enterprise to involve Guinness was the Dublin Exhibition Palace and Winter Garden Company, of which he was a director with William Dargan, the Duke of Leinster and other prominent Dublin citizens. The company was founded in 1862 with the intention of providing a permanent exhibition of Irish arts and manufactures and also reading rooms, flower gardens, and a gas-lit winter garden, for public enjoyment. Guinness negotiated personally for the site, that of the former Coburg Gardens behind St Stephen's Green south, and an architectural competition for the Exhibition Palace followed. Construction of the buildings began in 1863, to the designs of Alfred G Jones, and was hurried to a conclusion to accommodate an International Exhibition of Arts and Industries, which was opened by the Prince of Wales in May 1865. This proved a resounding success but the permanent exhibition of Irish products which followed met with public apathy. The Exhibition Company was unable to repay loans made for the construction of its buildings and in 1868 it foundered with debts of almost £50,000.[5]

Nevertheless, Benjamin Lee Guinness had been outstanding in his endeavours, both as a businessman and as a public figure, for Dublin and for Ireland as a whole. He was rewarded with a baronetcy in 1867.

In the year of Sir Benjamin Lee's death, 1868, the output of Guinness's brewery amounted to 350,411 barrels of porter.[6] During twenty-five years, production had quadrupled under his guidance, and the factory, covering four acres, had become the world's largest porter brewery. It was characteristic of Guinness's championship of Irish national endeavour that the harp of Brian Boru was adopted as the brewery's trade mark in 1862. He left an estate of £1,100,000, the largest ever proved in Ireland to that date.

By the terms of Sir Benjamin Lee Guinness's will, his house on St Stephen's Green passed to his youngest son, Edward Cecil Guinness (born 1847). The other main beneficiary was his eldest son, Arthur Edward Guinness (born 1840), who inherited the estate at Ashford, Co. Galway (bought by his father in 1855), a house called St Anne's at Clontarf, Co. Dublin, and the baronetcy.

Ownership of the brewery passed to the brothers jointly, but Sir Benjamin had been careful to lay down stringent conditions so as to prevent either partner from withdrawing and thereby depriving the company of half its capital. Ultimately, these conditions had to be overruled, as Sir Arthur had little interest in industry. In 1876, the partnership was dissolved, Sir Arthur receiving a cash payment of £680,000 and Edward became sole controller of the company, at the age of twenty-nine.[7] His business acumen had been clearly demonstrated in the years since 1868; profits had totalled over £1,500,000, of which some forty per cent was re-invested in the business. In the same period, Sir Arthur received a sum of £530,000 from the profits and Edward £385,000.[8] Edward consolidated his father's work, and, by 1880, the brewery was in a unique, unassailable commercial position. In 1886, it was turned into a limited company, and sold to the public for £6,000,000.

Sir Arthur and Edward Guinness inherited their father's generosity towards public works and, in 1870 they purchased the buildings and grounds of the Dublin Exhibition Palace Company for £60,000[9], thereby paying off the company's debts. In 1872, the buildings were used for an exhibition, which they sponsored jointly, of Irish arts and manufactures. This was attended with more controversy than success, for British labour was employed to refurbish the exhibition halls and, once opened, the display stands of the supposedly national exhibition were found to have been flooded with British goods.

Like the 1865 exhibition, the 1872 exhibition failed to promote a permanent display of Irish produce and the brothers were compared unfavourably by the press with their father, that great champion of national talent.[10] But both brothers continued over the years to give generous support to public works, notably with the reconstruction of the Coombe Lying-in Hospital and the remodelling of St Stephen's Green, which were financed by Sir Arthur, and the foundation of the Iveagh Trust by Edward Guinness in 1890 for the provision of artisan housing.[11]

In later years, Edward Guinness came to divide his time between London and Dublin. Besides the house on St Stephen's Green, he had bought a country house called Farmleigh in 1874, situated at the north-west corner of the Phoenix Park, and was often to be seen in the mornings walking across the Park to his office at the brewery. There was a town house in London, No. 5 Berkeley Street, and a country house in Suffolk, Elveden Hall, which was purchased from a maharaja. Edward Guinness was created a baronet in 1885 and, in 1891, a peer, taking his title from Iveagh in Co. Down. He became a viscount in 1905 and an earl in 1919.

The first Earl and Countess of Iveagh were particularly noted for the splendour of their entertaining, and it was said that their gatherings at St Stephen's Green came close to outshining those of the Lord Lieutenant himself[12]—which recalls similar observations made by Mrs Delany[13] on the stylish life of Dr and Mrs Clayton, a century and a half before.

The creation of the modern Iveagh House

In the second half of the 19th century, alterations and additions to the 18th-century house designed by Richard Castle transformed it into the Iveagh House of today. The process began in 1862, when Benjamin Lee Guinness acquired the leasehold of the house next door, No.81 St Stephen's Green.[1] This was dismantled, and its site used in 1866 to enlarge the Richard Castle house, in effect doubling its size (see plan, page 28). The original house and extension were given a unified façade of Portland stone, the one we see today. As at St Patrick's Cathedral, Guinness himself acted as the architect of the façade and of several very competent Georgian-style rooms inside.[2]

A second wave of alterations took place between 1880 and 1884 with additions on the other side of the Georgian building for Edward Guinness. J F Fuller was his architect and work began with the complete rebuilding of No.79 in 1880-1.[3] Where there had been a carriageway, Fuller constructed a link-building, with a first-floor corridor to the Georgian house. It seems certain that, at the same time, Fuller did away with Richard Castle's stairhall, with its single-return flight of stairs, and replaced it with the present splendid double-return staircase.[4] Finally, in 1884, No.78 was rebuilt to form a symmetrical pair with No.79.[5]

The effect of these alterations was to equip Guinness's town residence for lavish entertaining on the scale of a country house. A bachelors' wing had been created[6] and servants' rooms to house a staff of twenty. When the house was sold up in 1939, the sale catalogue listed twenty-three principal bedrooms and eleven bachelor's bedrooms.[7]

The choice of J F Fuller (1835-1924) as architect merits further comment. He was a pupil of the English architects, Alfred Waterhouse and M E Hadfield, and is one of the more eccentric talents in Irish architectural history, being well-known besides as a genealogist, novelist and antiquarian. In the 1870s, Fuller became the favourite architect of both Guinness brothers. From 1874 into the 1880s, he extended Farmleigh for Edward Guinness, in the Georgian style, as well as undertaking the work at St Stephen's Green.

His work for Sir Arthur was very extensive and costly, with commissions for creating a remarkable Italianate country mansion, St Anne's Clontarf (from 1873)[9], and adding a massive baronial castle to an existing house at Ashford, Co. Galway (where he replaced S N Roberts as architect in 1875).[10] Work on both these buildings continued into the 1880s, and he was also engaged to remodel Sir Arthur's Dublin house, No. 18 Lower Leeson Street, in 1875-6.[11] Fuller was in many respects the Victorian equivalent of Richard Castle, which makes his presence at Iveagh House historically appropriate.

The final addition to Iveagh House was the ballroom, a vast chamber capable of accommodating all resident and outside guests at one reception. It was designed in 1896 by the Glasgow-born architect, William Young (1843-1900), and its execution was supervised by the leading Irish architect, Sir Thomas Drew.[12] Young also designed a ballroom and some other apartments at Farmleigh in the same year, and additions to Elveden Hall executed between 1899 and 1903.

In the final years of the 19th century, Young was a noted exponent of the English classical manner. His masterpiece, the War Office, Whitehall, started in 1898 and completed in 1907 after his death, is in this style. The ballroom at Iveagh House is typical of his classical style, grandly public, though a little disappointing once the exuberant monumentality of the composition has been experienced. However, the ensemble at Iveagh House of stairhall, ballroom vestibule and ballroom is sumptuous, something worthy of the most glittering of Oscar Wilde's final acts.

5

ST.STEPHENS GREEN PARK. DUBLIN. 344.W.L.

The remodelling of St Stephen's Green

In tracing the history of Iveagh House up to the present day, it is appropriate to end as we began, by returning to its setting. For the public gardens of St Stephen's Green, which Iveagh House overlooks today, are very different in appearance from the rectangular meadow of Bishop Clayton's time—and this transformation was due to the enthusiasm and generosity of a member of the Guinness family.

By the end of the 18th century, St Stephen's Green had deteriorated in condition, so far that in 1792 the residents petitioned the Corporation—with little effect—to undertake improvements.[1] Aware of the need for drastic action, but also with a view to increasing city revenues, the Dublin Corporation appointed a committee to look into the future of St Stephen's Green. This reported in 1810[2], and suggested that the works should be financed by a lottery, which would raise a total of £50,000, to cover immediate improvements and annual repairs—and the construction of a new Mansion House in the centre of the square, an idea first put forward in 1792. But again nothing transpired. In 1814, a proposal to erect a testimonial to the Duke of Wellington—to replace Van Nost's statue of George II—was defeated, it being held that 'a king ought not to be removed to accommodate a subject'[3] In the same year, newspaper descriptions of the state of the Green indicate that it had reached its nadir, the outer wall punctuated with gaps, the drainage channel stagnant with rubbish, and the central greensward used for yeomanry exercises, and boxing matches.[4]

The solution adopted to the problems of St Stephen's Green was to close it to the public. This satisfied both the residents' desire for improvement and the Corporation's for extra revenue. At the end of 1814, Commissioners representing the householders of the area were empowered by Act of Parliament to take over the maintenance of the square, renting it from the Corporation for £300 per annum. The centre of the square was immediately remodelled at a cost of over £8,000. The ditch was filled in, French drains were laid and the old formal avenues replaced by gardens designed according to the principles of the Picturesque, with serpentine walks and clumps and spinneys of shrubs and evergreens. The gardens were enclosed by a high cast-iron railing with a broad gravel walk outside and, bordering the road, granite bollards linked by cast-iron chains. On the bollards, at sixty-yard intervals, were oil-lamps, the first attempt to provide public lighting in the square.[5] St Stephen's Green thus became a vast private park, accessible only to key-holders, at an annual rent of one guinea.

For more than half a century, use of the park remained the privilege of a few. But, submitted to the scrutiny of public-spirited Victorian eyes, a campaign was launched with the aim of converting the Green into a public facility worthy of a capital city. It began in the 1860s in The Dublin Builder, Ireland's leading architectural journal, but it was due to the intervention of Sir Arthur Guinness, elder son of Sir Benjamin Lee Guinness, that St Stephen's Green once more became a public park. In 1876, Guinness made a cash offer to the Commissioners, and, in 1877, the St Stephen's Green (Dublin) Act was passed at Westminster to facilitate the re-opening.[6]

Sir Arthur embarked on a scheme of remodelling with an enthusiasm which paralleled his father's in restoring St Patrick's Cathedral and at a personal cost of over £20,000. Helped by a civil engineer, A L Cousins, Sir Arthur designed much of the layout himself. An ornamental lake with a rockery cascade was created, fed by the Grand Canal at Portobello and drained at Huband Bridge. On either side of Van Nost's statue of George II, a fountain was installed surrounded by formal flowerbeds. J F Fuller designed a keeper's lodge and 'Swiss' shelters.[7] St Stephen's Green was opened to the public, without ceremony, on 27 July, 1880.

Since its re-opening, St Stephen's Green has been maintained by the Commissioners of Public Works and has changed remarkably little. A statue of Sir Arthur Guinness, Lord Ardilaun, by Thomas Farrell, was erected in 1892. In 1894, the planting was completed with one hundred witch elms along the outer walks. The main alterations to the park since

then have been to its gallery of sculptures—
George II was removed in the 1920s and other
works have balanced its disappearance.
Though St Stephen's Green almost gained a
municipal gallery of art designed by Sir
Edwin Lutyens—the west side of the gardens being
proposed as a site in 1913[8]—it seems that for once
the loss to architecture may have been the city's
gain. For the survival in its completeness, of *the
spacious area*' praised by Malton, gives Dublin one
of her chief glories.

6

Iveagh House in the present century

The second Earl of Iveagh. A copy of the portrait in oils by H A Olivier.

In Ireland, as in the other countries of Europe, the years of the First World War were ones of violent and profound change, which permanently altered the nation's social and political life. In 1922, Ireland achieved political independence and the traditions of Vice-Regal society came to an end. But the buildings which had formed the setting for the pre-war world lingered on, many to be destroyed or to suffer a slower death by misuse and decay. Lord Iveagh's Dublin town house was more fortunate than many in surviving intact and unharmed, but its functional relevance had waned with social change.

Though the first Earl of Iveagh maintained his charitable and industrial activities in Ireland in the 1920s, he had been deeply distressed by the 1916 Rising and subsequent political upheavals and spent his later years for the most part in England. He died in 1927 and was succeeded by his eldest son, Rupert Edward Cecil Guinness.

The second Earl of Iveagh (1874-1967) had been an active member of Parliament at Westminster for many years and this, coupled with the expansion of the Guinness brewery's trade in Britain, meant that much of his time was spent away from Ireland. His family continued to use their two Dublin residences, however—the house on St Stephen's Green and Farmleigh—until the late 1930s, when the Earl made the munificent offer of his town house and its gardens to the Irish nation. The offer was formally accepted on 19 May 1939 by the Taoiseach, Eamon de Valera. A sale of the contents was held at the end of September.

Following its presentation to the nation, the house was officially named Iveagh House by the Government and, in December 1939, was allocated to the Department of External Affairs (re-named in 1969 the Department of Foreign Affairs). Few alterations were required by the building's new function, other than an office wing which was added to the rear in 1949. It continues the line of the old bachelors' corridor on the east side of the garden and was designed by W H Howard Cooke, Deputy Principal Architect at the Office of Public Works 1943-7. In the early 1950s a scheme of refurnishing was carried out under the direction of the distinguished Principal Architect at the Office of Public Works, Raymond McGrath. The most important feature of the work was a fine set of Donegal carpets, designed by Raymond McGrath in 1952-3 for the inner hall, stairhall, old music-room, saloon, drawing-room and, most spectacularly, the ballroom. This was Mr McGrath's first major commission as a designer of carpets and he was soon to become famous for his work in this field.

The suitability of Iveagh for its modern rôle is witnessed not only by the continuing splendour of its historic fabric but also by the way its use as a centre for important receptions has endured. To the old tradition of society gatherings a political dimension has been added and numerous distinguished politicians and heads of state have visited the building, including many in recent years from Ireland's partner countries in the European Economic Community.

7

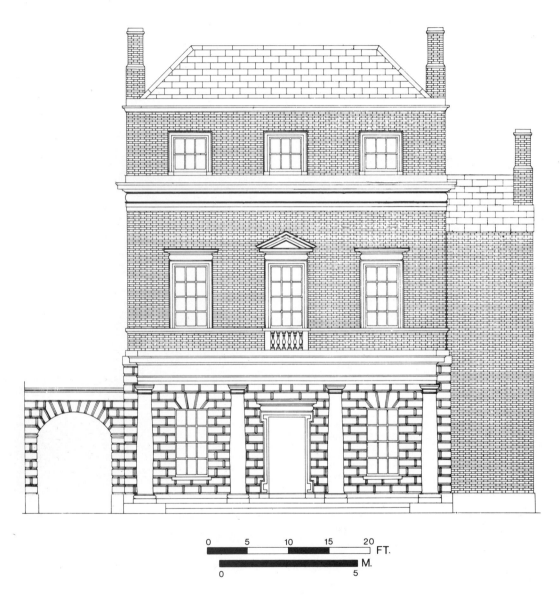

7. *Bishop Clayton's house: a reconstruction of the façade erected in 1736 to the designs of Richard Castle.*
In designing this elevation, Castle employed a geometric system of proportions based on a square of 40ft. and its quarters.
8. *Iveagh House, the entrance front. A modern view of the façade erected in 1866 to the designs of Sir Benjamin Lee Guinness.*

0 5 10 15 20 FT.
0   5   M.

Description of the house

8

The exterior

The façade of Iveagh House was erected in 1866 with Benjamin Lee Guinness acting as his own architect. Its design is a close imitation of Aldborough House, Portland Row, Dublin, a town mansion of the 1790s. Guinness's choice of a Georgian style in the mid-Victorian period must reflect his personal tastes, but is also faithful to the general Italianism which pervades much Irish architecture of the 18th and 19th centuries.

The exterior (plate 8) achieves elegance through the silvery smoothness of its Portland stone and the precision of its detail. Behind the three leftmost bays of the façade stands the 1736 house. The design's weakest point – the awkwardly tall first-floor – results from the 18th-century saloon inside, with its lofty coved ceiling. Richard Castle had skilfully concealed this (see plate 7) , by placing the main cornice at second-floor level, rather than at roof level as Guinness does.

The façade is crowned by a pediment containing the arms of Sir Benjamin Lee Guinness's baronetcy with his motto, *Spes mea in Deo.* Also noteworthy is the cast-iron railing at street level (plate 8), a richly-modelled foliage scroll which dates, with the splendid cast-iron lanterns flanking the portico, from 1866.

To the left of Iveagh House are Nos. 79 and 78 St Stephen's Green, built to J F Fuller's designs in 1881 and 1884 respectively. They are in a rather crude neo-Georgian style of red brick dressed with red sandstone. Much more accomplished is Fuller's two-storeyed link building of 1880 between No. 79 and Iveagh House, where panels are skilfully let into the exterior to conceal changes of level within.

9. Ground-floor plan.
10. First-floor plan.

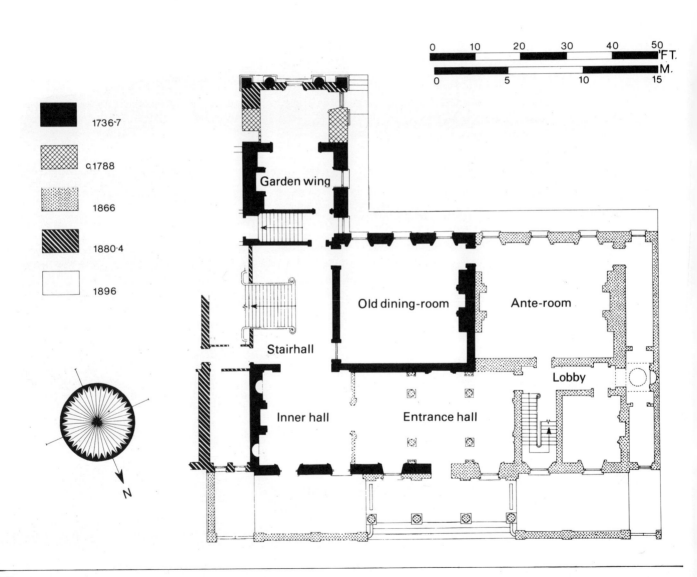

1736-7

c.1788

1866

1880-4

1896

Garden wing

Stairhall

Old dining-room

Ante-room

Lobby

Inner hall

Entrance hall

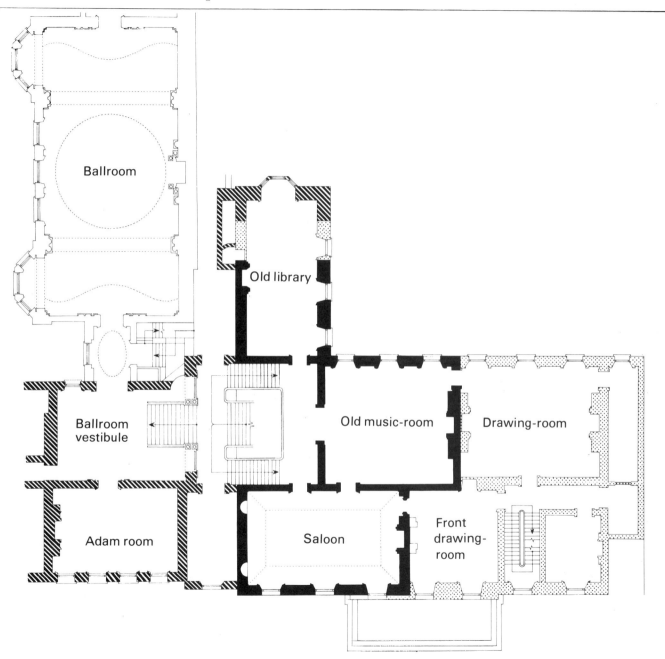

Ballroom

Old library

Ballroom vestibule

Old music-room

Drawing-room

Adam room

Saloon

Front drawing-room

11

1. *The entrance hall, with the inner hall beyond.*
2. *Wooden bas-relief panel in the entrance hall:* Priam entreats Achilles to release the body of Hector.
3. *Wooden bas-relief panel in the entrance hall:* Achilles plays his lyre.

The entrance hall

The entrance hall of Iveagh House (plate 11) was created in 1866. It is approached through the Doric entrance portico, and this columnar theme is continued inside by two Ionic screens which run across the width of the room. The style of the room is Georgian, but no specific reference point has been chosen and decorative features of the early 1700s are mixed with ones from the 1750s and 1770s. Since the Office of Public Works took over maintenance of the building, the oak wall-panelling has been painted to lighten the room.

Four 19th-century sculptures furnish the entrance hall, all purchased by Benjamin Lee Guinness at the Dublin Exhibition of 1865. To the right of the main door is *The Letter,* dated 1865, by Antonio Tantardini, a Milanese sculptor. At the opposite end of the room are two busts by the Roman sculptor G B Lombardi, on the left, *Joy,* dated 1864, and on the right, *Modesty,* a veiled bust, dated 1863. Opposite the main door is the most accomplished of the four subjects, *The Sleeping Faun and Satyr* by the American sculptress Harriet Hosmer. This was one of the most admired of the 1865 exhibits and its purchase price was £1,000.[1]

The most interesting objects in the room are two wooden bas-relief panels mounted on the inner wall. Though their frames date from 1866, they are the work of an 18th-century sculptor. Two scenes from the Iliad are depicted, on the left *King Priam of Troy, conducted by Hermes to the Myrmidon encampment, entreats Achilles to release the body of his slain son, Hector* (plate 12)[2] and on the right, *In the Myrmidon encampment, Achilles, playing his lyre, and Patroclus, are approached by Aias and Odysseus* (plate 13).[3] The provenance of the panels is mysterious. They may have formed part of the *"...very fine high carving..."* seen by Mrs Pendarves in the Bishop's first house in 1731. Or they may be fittings from the 1736 Richard Castle house – perhaps overmantels for twin fireplaces in the first-floor saloon. If the latter is the case, they may have come from the workshop of John Houghton, a sculptor who worked frequently in Castle's retinue of craftsmen.

12

13

14

4. *The Shepherd Boy Sculpture in white marble by John Hogan, 1846.*
5. *Carved wooden chimney-piece in the inner hall.*

The inner hall

To walk from the entrance hall to the inner hall brings us into the 18th-century part of Iveagh House (see plate 9). The inner hall still owes its character to Richard Castle and, before the alterations of 1866, it served the purpose for which it had been designed in 1736, that of an entrance hall. Guinness's enlargement of the building made it an adjunct to the stairhall, but the 18th-century arrangement can readily be understood by visiting No. 85 St Stephen's Green, designed by Castle two years after Bishop Clayton's house to a very similar plan. The inner hall at Iveagh House and the hall at No. 85 also share common decorative features – a cornice with robust and simple modillions, and vigorously framed wall-panelling.

The semi-circular niches on either side of the chimney-piece are probably to Castle's design, though their frames would seem to date from 1866. They contain, on the left, a figure of Mercury, from the studio of Bertel Thorwaldsen, the Danish neo-Classical sculptor and, on the right, another exhibit from the 1865 exhibition, *Modesty,* by the Milanese sculptor Quintilio Corbellini.[4]

The wooden chimney-piece (plate 15) is of great interest. Its upper half is 18th-century work, with a bas-relief panel depicting a scene of sacrifice, probably that described in the first book of the Iliad, *The Achaeans offering a sacrifice of bulls and goats to Apollo.* This can be associated with the two larger panels seen in the entrance hall. The frame of the panel is borrowed directly from a published design by William Kent, for a chimney-piece in the stone hall at Houghton Hall, Norfolk.[5] The fire surround below the mantelshelf is a 19th-century neo-Palladian design, probably by J F Fuller, c. 1880.[6]

Against the wall facing the fireplace is the finest piece of sculpture in the Iveagh House collection, the reclining figure of a shepherd boy (plate 14) by John Hogan. Hogan, (1800-1858) was Ireland's greatest neo-Classical sculptor, a native of Cork who worked for many years in Rome. *The Shepherd Boy* is signed and dated 1846. Its Arcadian theme is depicted with remarkable and touching realism; the

15

suggestion of weight in the reclining body is especially convincing. This splendid work was formerly in the Ardilaun collection at St Anne's Clontarf. When a sale of the contents was held in 1939, Hogan's sculpture was purchased by Mr John Burke, a Dublin solicitor, who presented it to the nation.

The two other sculptures in the room are a bust of Sir Benjamin Lee Guinness, executed in 1851 by the Irish sculptor Christopher Moore, and an unsigned mid-19th-century genre piece depicting a Roman youth.

A wide opening flanked by Ionic pilasters, created in 1866, connects the inner hall with the stairhall. At the foot of the stairs stands another 19th-century genre sculpture, *The reading Girl* (plate 16) by the Milanese sculptor Pietro Magni, a purchase from the 1865 exhibition[7].

The garden wing of the house is entered from the stairhall. Here, an 18th-century cabinet-room survives, much altered, with an excellent grey marble chimney-piece in Richard Castle's style (plate 3), which probably came from elsewhere in the house, and an attractive plaster frieze of the late 1760s.

16

The old dining-room
Adjacent to the stairhall, this room is part of the 18th-century building and was probably used originally as a dining-room. It retains much of its authentic character (plate 17), with vigorously shouldered wall-panelling, similar to that in the inner hall, and splendid door-cases. However, the door to the left of the chimney-breast, leading to the extension added by Benjamin Lee Guinness, dates from 1866, and so do the windows.

The chimney-piece is partly original. Its frieze is another example of the fine 18th-century wood-carving seen in the house. It has a charming and delicate motif of *putti* making wine and a centrepiece representing the drunken Silenus, copied by its carver from an engraving of a Rubens painting.[8] This is probably the frieze of the room's original chimney-piece, for its theme is suited to a dining-room, but it has been shortened, and incorporated into a rather coarse neo-Georgian fire surround, probably by J F Fuller, c. 1880.

The most beautiful feature of the room is its ornamental plaster frieze. Like other decorative plasterwork at Iveagh House, this would seem to post-date the construction of Bishop Clayton's house in 1736, for its naturalistic precision has little in common with the more generalized Baroque style of plasterwork in other Richard Castle houses. It seems logical that it is late rococo work, installed after Viscount Mountcashel bought the house in 1766. To instal fashionable new plasterwork decorations was a means of up-dating an existing building and is something which apparently happened frequently in Irish 18th-century houses of both town and country. The frieze is extremely delicately modelled (plate 18), and each wall of the room is treated differently. Among the motifs are roses, tulips, swags of laurel leaves, shells, and, in three of the four corners, bunches of grapes, again suggesting a former use as a dining-room.

16. *The reading Girl Sculpture in white marble by Pietro Magni, mid-19th century.*
17. *The old dining-room.*

18

20

1

. Detail of ornamental plaster frieze in the old dining-room.
. Door-case in the ante-room.
. Detail of carved wooden frieze of the old dining-room chimney-piece.

The ante-room

The door from the old dining-room brings us from the 18th-century house into the 1866 extension. The ante-room is in neo-Georgian style, its ceiling inspired by that of the Provost's House at Trinity College, a building begun in 1759. But like the 1866 entrance hall, this room jumbles together features from different phases of Georgian architecture and swan-necked door pediments, imitating mid-18th-century examples, are incorporated with bolection wall-panelling of an early 18th-century type.

Two notable features of the room recur elsewhere in the house. First, the beautiful engraved brass lock-plates (plate 28), with pendant door-handles and a central slide concealing the keyhole. These must be fittings from the 1736 house, displaced in 1866 and moved to the extension. The second feature is the fan-moulding seen on the window architraves, between shutter and lintel, a common detail in late 18th- and early 19th-century Irish window joinery.

The door on the long inside wall of the ante-room leads into a Victorian lobby, arranged so as to give a vista to a small domed vestibule, in which stands a statuary group of Jupiter and Juno, a copy after Bernini. The lobby abounds in the pre-cast plaster mouldings so often found in Victorian classical interiors. A back staircase with a cast-iron balustrade leads to the top floor of the house. The lobby leads back into the entrance hall.

The stairhall

This palatial room (plate 21) is one of the most memorable of Irish 19th-century interiors. But though its design is Victorian, its fabric is a conglomeration of the work of different periods, as is the case in most of the rooms at Iveagh House. The stairhall of today is not the one designed by Richard Castle. His design must have subdivided the present room into two, one part housing the main stairs— a single-return flight only—and the other part housing a separate service stair. This is the arrangement of staircases seen at No. 85 St Stephen's Green.

It seems clear, both from stylistic evidence and the surviving documentation, that J F Fuller completely remodelled the stairhall in 1881 and created the double-return staircase we see today.[9] It is a splendid mahogany construction, which skilfully re-uses Castle's wrought-iron balustrade (plates 23 and 24) interspersing the original balusters with copies. The original fretwork risers are similarly re-used and the fine carved frontispiece to the landing lintel (plate 25) is again 18th-century work.
On the first-floor landing are three doors designed by Fuller, the central one carved entertainingly with tropical designs — on its right-hand fold, a mahogany snake is devouring a frog.

The double staircase was created at the same time as Fuller was remodelling No. 79 next door. The ceiling of the stairhall is skilfully lit by two circular skylights fitted into the narrow gap between the houses. The ceiling plasterwork (plate 22) mixes rococo and neo-Classical motifs in typical Fuller manner. However, the panelling of the walls, in onyx and alabaster, must be work of 1896 to William Young's designs, matching the decorative scheme of the ballroom. The triple-arched screen leading to the ballroom, and the two rusticated arches on the half-landing, must also be due to Young. In fact the ballroom forms a much more appropriate termination to the great staircase than does the 18th-century part of the house, for both stairhall and ballroom are in a very public style. They are at their most handsome at night in the artificial blaze of chandeliers.

21

The stairhall with the ballroom vestibule beyond, seen from the first-floor landing.
The stairhall ceiling.

23

24

25

The old music-room

This extremely elegant apartment (plate 26), entered from a door on the first-floor landing, is part of the 1736 house. It must have served as a more intimate drawing-room alongside the large, formal saloon with which it interconnects.

The door-cases (plate 34) are coeval with the room. They display Richard Castle's design at its best – masculine and assertive, each line charged with energy. The architrave is massively framed and shouldered, and broken through by a dentil cornice. The wood is West Indian mahogany of the highest quality, used to lavish advantage by its joiner. This material had only become generally used in Ireland in the late 1720s and Castle was among its champions. He used it in Dublin at Leinster House and Tyrone House and at Russborough, Co. Wicklow. But as these buildings post-date Bishop Clayton's house, the Iveagh House doors may be his first use of the material. The doors retain their original engraved brass lock-plates (plate 28).

The most important feature of the room is its ceiling (plate 27) which must date, like the frieze in the old dining-room below, from after 1766.[10] Its design is transitional. Rococo animation is frozen and its forms are governed by a tranquil poise which anticipates the neo-classical style of the 1770s. The ceiling is basically symmetrical in design. It bears musical instruments suggestive of chamber music – a French horn, a recorder, a flute, and musical books. The room was probably used for music-making in the 18th century, and at the time of the 1939 sale was known as a music room. The intertwining arabesques, swags of flowers, and trilling birds are typical of earlier Dublin rococo work, and the frieze (plate 33), as in the room below, is treated differently on each wall. The modelling of the plasterwork is admirably shallow and elegant.

The insertion of the ceiling was only the first of several remodellings of the room. In 1866, new windows were installed and a door was driven through the wall on the left of the chimney-piece. About 1880, Fuller inserted an Adam-style fireplace, replaced in the 1960s by an elegant fireplace of

23. The ground-floor curtail of the staircase.
24. Central wrought-iron panel of the staircase landing.
25. Detail of the carved wooden frontispiece to the staircase landing.
26. The old music-room.

26

c. 1790 (plate 32). The carpet, in a floral Baroque style, was designed by Raymond McGrath in 1953.

The room contains three fine paintings of classical ruins, by the Irish artist George Barret, which must date from the third quarter of the 18th century: opposite the windows, *The ruins of the Forum at Rome* (plate 29); and on the left of the double door, *A view of Tivoli and the Temple of Vesta* (plate 30), and on the right, *The ruins of the Coliseum (plate 31).*

29

27. *Detail of the ceiling plasterwork of the old music-room.*

28 *Brass door furniture in the old music-room.*

Three classical landscapes in oils by George Barret, in the old music-room;

29 *The ruins of the Forum at Rome;*

30 *View of Tivoli and the Temple of Vesta;*

31 *The ruins of the Coliseum.*

27

30

28

31

32. Chimney-piece in the old music-room.
33. Detail of ornamental plaster frieze in the old music-room.
34. Door-case in the old music-room.

32

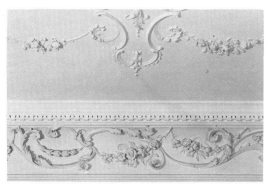

33

34

35

5. *The saloon.*
6. *The saloon ceiling.*

The saloon

This was the *'great room'* so much admired by Lord Orrery in 1736 (see page 16).In Bishop Clayton's day, it was a saloon — a formal drawing-room — and its original function is matched by the architectural grandeur of its decorations. Today, it remains largely as Richard Castle designed it.

The Iveagh House saloon was the prototype for two of the finest rooms in Irish architectural history, the saloons at No. 85 St Stephen's Green and Carton, Co. Kildare. Both probably date from the same year, 1739, and are decorated with magnificent Baroque plasterwork by the Francini brothers. By contrast, the Iveagh House saloon of 1736, which probably pre-dates the arrival of the Francini brothers in Ireland, is decorated with a classical restraint which is close to the manner of some English Palladian architects - notably William Kent, whose saloon at No. 44 Berkeley Square, London (1745), parallels Bishop Clayton's. In decorating the deep cove of the saloon ceiling, Richard Castle used square, cross-shaped and octagonal coffers modelled in perspective (plate 36), adapted from a plate in one of his favourite works of reference, Serlio's *Five Books of Architecture,* showing the coffering of the Temple of Bacchus in Rome.[11]

On the east wall of the room are two semi-circular coffered niches. It seems that, as at No. 85 St Stephen's Green, there were two more niches on the opposite wall, which presumably were filled in during the 1866 remodelling. Probably the original arrangement in the two houses was to have a fireplace on both end walls of the saloon, flanked on either side by niches. Also identical to the arrangement at No. 85 is the pairing of the doors on the inside wall of the saloon, one door opening into the adjoining old music-room, the other opening on to the landing. This skilful arrangement enables the first-floor reception rooms to interconnect, while preserving the symmetry of the saloon.
The saloon doors are of mahogany to the same design as in the old music-room and the mahogany dado is also original. The rest of the woodwork is Victorian, the windows dating from 1866 and the fireplace from 1880.

The front drawing-room

A door from the saloon, driven through the outside wall of the 18th-century house, leads into this neo-Georgian room of 1866. It has an ornamental plaster frieze, a rather mechanical imitation of rococo scrollwork,and Palladian-style door architraves. The finest feature of the room is its Victorian chimney-piece, resplendent in dark green marble and polished cast-iron.

36

37

*The drawing-room.
Chimney-piece in the
drawing-room.
Door-case in the
drawing-room.*

The drawing-room

Entered from a door on the left of the first-floor lobby, this is the most ambitious of the neo-Georgian interiors executed during Benjamin Lee Guinness's extensions of 1866. Like the ante-room below, the drawing-room (plate 37) has decorations inspired by the early 1760s dining-room at the Provost's House, Trinity College: there is the same dado rail carved with a wave pattern, and the same diagonally-coffered ceiling. Yet the dainty elegance of the Provost's room has not been captured. The reason lies in the very Victorianism of the imitation, and the desire to improve on – as well as to simulate – an 18th-century scheme.

The ornamentation of the doors and panelling (plate 39) is in plaster, where an 18th-century craftsman would have used wood, and the decorative plasterwork of the ceiling is rather lifeless on close examination. Some of the decorative features are anachronistic — small baronial shields above the fireplaces, pendants to the ceiling coffers, Grecian lily-leaf mouldings to the door-frames — and a slightly cluttered atmosphere replaces the airiness of the Provost's room. Yet, on first acquaintance, the room is convincingly mid-Georgian — so convincing that the writers of the *Georgian Society Records* of 1909-13 included it in their second volume.[12]

Besides its 18th-century style, the drawing-room has that atmosphere of comfort and intimacy which is one of the most pleasant qualities of Victorian interior design. In former days, this must have been a charming family room. There are two particularly attractive features – the six tapestry panels on the inner wall, depicting 18th-century couples in tree-lined groves, in the manner of the painters Watteau and Pater, and the two chimney-pieces (plate 38) in neo-Palladian style, their central panels depicting *putti* with the symbols, respectively of music and geography. The floral Baroque-style carpet was designed by Raymond McGrath; its pattern reflecting the design of the ceiling.

38

39.

The old library

This room, entered from the first-floor landing, is in the garden wing of the house, and has a decorative scheme dating basically from 1866. It has bolection wall-panelling in oak (plate 40), and an imitation rococo frieze like that in the front drawing-room. The frieze is not symmetrical, however, as it ought to be, suggesting that the room was extended in length by J F Fuller, c. 1881, and that he installed the oriel window and neo-Palladian bookcases.

The most interesting feature of the room is the chimney-piece (plate 41). The pediment is crowned by the arms of Sir Benjamin Lee Guinness, but the fire-surround and upper frame must be another of Fuller's neo-Georgian designs. The wooden bas-relief panel dates from the 18th century and, like the three panels seen on the ground floor, draws its subject from Homer's Iliad. It depicts a scene from the sixth book, *Hector's parting with Andromache at the gate of Troy, before leaving for battle against the Achaeans.*

40

Oak panelling and door-case in the old library.
Carved wooden chimney-piece in the old library.
The Adam room.

The ballroom vestibule

The vestibule is reached by steps which ascend from the half-landing on the main staircase. The site chosen for the construction of Lord Iveagh's ballroom in 1896 was the garden at the rear of No. 79 St Stephen's Green and half of the first floor of No. 79 itself was turned into the ballroom vestibule. Like the stairhall, the ballroom vestibule is panelled *en suite* with the ballroom in onyx and alabaster. On the far wall, a jib-door on the left leads through the thickness of the wall into No.78. On the side wall is a classical doorway in the Mannerist style, designed by William Young.

The monumental wooden seat on the far wall should be noted. It is an imitation of a late 16th-century Italian *cassapanca* (a sofa and chest combined). Above the seat are three carved panels, the centre one depicting Bacchus and Ariadne, and these may be further examples of the 18th-century wood-carving seen in the house.

The Adam room

This charming room (plate 42) adjoining the ballroom vestibule pre-dates William Young's alterations and is part of J F Fuller's work of 1881. It is of special interest in being decorated in the Adam style of the late 18th century. In the last quarter of the 19th century, the Adam style was revived with some success, and firms such as Gillows, or Sibthorpe and Son in Dublin, supplied whole 'Adam' interiors.[13] It seems likely that this room was fitted up to order by a furnishing firm such as Sibthorpes. It is an excellent example of the type, but like other examples of the revival, it owes as much to French *Louis seize* interiors as to the brothers Adam. The most authentic 'Adam' feature is the decorative plasterwork of the ceiling, from the centre of which hangs an excellent Victorian glass chandelier.

42

43

The ballroom.

The ballroom

The ballroom is a fitting conclusion to a description of Iveagh House. It was the last of the great rooms to be constructed and, at 60 feet by 35 feet by 40 feet high, is also the largest. It was designed by William Young in 1896 and is typical of his classical style at its most ostentatious. It is a vast chamber, public in scale and furnishings, the walls awash with polychromatic panels of Algerian onyx in Carrara marble and Irish alabaster frames. The room is built to a tripartite plan, the centre dominated by a dome, and the overall effect is rather like some vast and magnificent *tepidarium* of the ancients. It is said to have cost more than £30,000.[14]

The design of the room mixes many stylistic sources. The marbled walls are inspired by 18th-century interiors, perhaps ones at Versailles or at Holkham or Houghton in Norfolk. But much of the decorative detail in the room is in the Italian Mannerist style of the late 16th century. This style is seen particularly in the two great semicircular panels of plasterwork on the walls beneath the dome (plate 44) where two symmetrical figures, one bearing a lute, the other a tambourine, are set amidst tendrils of foliage and strapwork which sprout, beneath a central cartouche, a bearded head and feathered wings. The plasterwork in the room was executed by the firm of Darcy and was praised in its time[15] for returning to the technique of stucco modelling *in situ,* rather than relying on pre-cast ornament. However, on close inspection, it is clear that though the work is indeed hand-finished, moulds dictated the basic forms.

The two-tier chimney-piece (plate 44) facing the windows is notable. It follows the revived Elizabethan fireplace fashion established by the English architect Richard Norman Shaw, but the alabaster chosen for the execution of the design has deficiencies as a material. As on the engaged alabaster columns around the walls, the detailing of the chimney-piece is inexpressive, rather like chiselled soap.

The Iveagh House ballroom is not only remarkable for its size, but also for the completeness of its furnishings. The most splendid feature is the set of window hangings, executed by Morrison of Edinburgh[16] – cherry-red damask is overlaid with strapwork outlines in dark red velvet and gold thread, and *appliqué* sprays of flowers embroidered in silk. The built-in seat furniture is original too, in French *régence* style, and delightful bays, for 'sitting out' from dances are provided at either end of the room (plate 45).

In each corner of the room there is a fine candelabrum in neo-classical style on pedestals veneered with porphry and malachite. Bronze figures, two of Mercury and two of Iris, bear the candelabra, and are signed by Giuseppe Boschi, Rome, 1806 and 1807. The carpet is modern, executed in 1952 to the designs of Raymond McGrath. Its design is based on marine motifs, with riverine heads adapted from those ornamenting the Custom House in Dublin.

The metal-work balustrades to the galleries of the ballroom are of aluminium as in the ballroom vestibule, in a style similar to that of the late 17th-century wrought-iron artist, Jean Tijou. The metal is rather flashy in appearance, but sensitively worked—a characteristic expression of the faith of Victorians in the materials of their age.
The *Irish Builder* provides an amusing footnote concerning the metal-work, for the apparently massive fireplace fender proved to be "*. . . so light that the host, when showing it to a guest, was seen to take it up in one hand"!* The room's other great innovation was a carefully concealed system of electric lighting.

Less than thirty years after its construction, with the passing of Vice-Regal society, the great ballroom at Iveagh House had become an anachronism. It is doubly fortunate, therefore, that it survived intact until 1939 and has been impeccably cared for since then. It has found an entirely suitable new use for Government receptions and conferences and for the conferring of honorary degrees. And in its splendour, it continues to remind us of the palmy days of the early 1900s.

44

Chimney-piece and
ornamental
plasterwork in the
ballroom.
An end bay in the
ballroom.

45

Iveagh Gardens

Iveagh Gardens are among the finest and the least-known of all Dublin's parks and gardens. They lie on a site south of St Stephen's Green, between Earlsfort Terrace and Harcourt Street, screened on all four sides by houses and secluded from the noise of the city. Little has changed here for over a century, which would be remarkable for any garden, but is particularly so for one in the centre of a modern capital.

The land on which the gardens were laid out was nothing more than a patchwork of open fields in Bishop Clayton's day, despite the energetic building development taking place nearby on St Stephen's Green and around Aungier Street. By the 1750s, the area had been named Leeson's Fields after the celebrated Dublin brewer Joseph Leeson, later first Earl of Milltown.

Not until 1777, with the laying-out of a new street from the south-west corner of St Stephen's Green, was a finger of invasion pointed at Leeson's Fields. The new street was Harcourt Street and, in 1778, its first major house was completed, for Jack Scott, first Earl of Clonmel, a prominent but disreputable Dublin lawyer.[1] Scott must have wanted to create the illusion of a country house on the verge of the city, for he bought up eleven acres of Leeson's Fields to serve as the gardens to his house. Thereafter, the land became known as Lord Clonmel's Lawn[2] and, when the new street intervened between the house and the garden, a tunnel was dug under the road to link them. Clonmel House still stands, though without the wings which originally flanked it.

The first Earl of Clonmel died in 1798 and his son spent little time in Ireland. In 1817, the gardens were leased, re-named Coburg Gardens and opened to the public. They enjoyed an all too brief vogue and, in 1836, reverted to Thomas, Earl of Clonmel. At this point, the gardens narrowly escaped building development; plans were drawn up for a new street, to be lined with town houses and named—predictably enough—Clonmel Street. It was to run parallel to the south side of St Stephen's Green, across the site of Coburg Gardens, to a junction with Harcourt Street. The scheme received the imprimatur of the Wide Streets Commissioners in 1837[3] but in the event was never begun.

It was not until 1862 that the ". . . *uneven, trampled, and most anti-picturesque Coburg Gardens*"[4] were once more taken in hand. Benjamin Lee Guinness saw in them an ideal site for the Dublin Exhibition Palace and bought them from John Henry, Earl of Clonmel.[5] In April 1863, Guinness leased them to the Dublin Exhibition Palace and Winter Garden Company, by which time a complete remodelling for public use was well-advanced, under the directions of the landscape architect Ninian Niven.[6]

Niven's pleasure gardens were approached from the Exhibition Palace through the winter garden, which was housed in a glass and iron conservatory running the entire length of the rear of the building, and which had a semicircular 'transept' leading to the outdoors. Just as a Victorian architect might express his enthusiasm for the styles of various epochs and nationalities in bricks and mortar, so Niven did here in his lawns and rockeries. The main parterre was laid out in the Italian style with formal flowerbeds and two fountains, while the southern part of the gardens was laid out in 'the American style'[7] with rhododendrons and curious rocky outcrops. Adjoining this was a miniature maze, inspired by the Tudor maze at Hampton Court in London, and to the west, distracting the eye from the rear façades of the houses on Harcourt Street, was a rustic grotto, twenty feet high, crowned by a fountain. But the real novelty of the whole scheme was the three-acre archery ground—used to great effect during the International Exhibition of 1865, with both ladies and gentlemen competing. This diverting by-product of Victorian neo-Mediaevalism still survives, as do many of the other features of Niven's layout.

The small pavilion (plate 46) built of Bath stone, in the private garden of Iveagh House also dates from those days. It was designed as a centrepiece for a small lake, which was needed to provide the water supply for the fountains of the pleasure gardens. In both setting and style, it was a conscious piece of

Iveagh Gardens

6. *Stone pavilion in the garden of Iveagh House.*

Celtic revivalism, imitating in miniature the oratory on the Isle of Inisfallen in Co. Kerry.[8] The pavilion was built in 1863, probably to the designs of Benjamin Lee Guinness himself.

With the failure of the Exhibition Palace Company, the gardens and buildings were re-acquired in 1870 by the Guinness family.[9] The exhibition of 1872 again failed to establish permanent public access to the site and the gardens returned to private ownership. In 1883, Edward Guinness sold the exhibition buildings to the Commissioners of Public Works to be adapted to house the new Royal University, the gardens remaining the property of the Guinness family. The buildings were further adapted after the creation of University College, Dublin in

1908, and in 1918 the present façade to Earlsfort Terrace was erected to the designs of R M Butler.

In 1939, the Earl of Iveagh presented Iveagh House to the nation. Iveagh Gardens—the grounds of the old Exhibition Palace—were presented to University College and, in 1941, were reunited with the college buildings of Earlsfort Terrace.
For almost thirty years, the gardens were used as never before, as a communication between the modern university buildings and those of Newman's rectorate. But with the departure of University College for a more spacious setting outside the city, the gardens are empty once more. It is to be hoped that one day they will again enjoy the popularity they deserve.

46

Appendix

List of occupants of Iveagh House

1736 *Dr Robert Clayton,* Bishop of Cork and (from 1745)
Clogher. Clayton commissioned the building of the
house, 1736-7, to Richard Castle's designs. Clayton
died in 1758 and his widow, *Catherine Clayton,*
remained in the house until her death in 1766.

1767 *Stephen, second Viscount Mountcashel,* created
first Earl of Mountcashel, 1781. Died 1790. *Countess
Mountcashel* remained in the house until her death
in 1792, after which it passed to their son, *Stephen,
second Earl of Mountcashel,* who sold the house in
1807.

1809 *John Philpot Curran,* Master of the Rolls

1814 *Sir William McMahon,* Master of the Rolls

1819 *Charles Burton,* later (1820) Justice of the King's
Bench. Burton remained in the house until his death
in 1847, after which it passed to his son-in-law
Robert Beatty West. After West's death, the house
passed to the *Commissioners of Encumbered
Estates,* who re-sold it.

1856 *Benjamin Lee Guinness,* later (1867) first baronet.
Taking over the site of No. 81 St Stephen's Green,
Guinness enlarged the house in 1866. He died in
1868 and the house passed to his youngest son,
Edward Cecil Guinness, later baronet, peer, first
Viscount Iveagh, and (1919) first Earl of Iveagh.
Having purchased the sites of Nos. 78 and 79 St.
Stephen's Green, he extended the house, 1880-4,
and in 1896 constructed the ballroom. He died in
1927, and the house passed to his son, *Rupert,
second Earl of Iveagh.* In May 1939, Lord Iveagh
presented the house to the Irish nation.

1939 *The Department of External Affairs*
List of Ministers for External Affairs since 1939
(1939) The Taoiseach, Eamon de Valera
1948 Seán MacBride
1951 Frank Aiken
1954 Liam Cosgrave
1957 Frank Aiken
(1969 Department re-named *The Department of
Foreign Affairs*)
1969 Patrick Hillery
1973 (Jan.-Feb.) Brian Lenihan
1973 Garret FitzGerald
1977 Michael O'Kennedy

List of plates with acknowledgements

All the photographs listed below, with the exception of those otherwise credited, were taken by Mr James Bambury, Senior Photographer at the Office of Public Works, Dublin.

1. St Stephen's Green, Dublin. From the etching by James Malton published in 1796. By courtesy of the Chester Beatty Library. (Photo: Pieterse Davison International).
2. Bishop Clayton and his wife. From the double portrait in oils by James Latham. By courtesy of the Representative Church Body. (Photo: National Gallery of Ireland).
3. Marble chimney-piece on the ground-floor of the garden wing. Drawn by Nicholas Sheaff.
4. Sir Benjamin Lee Guinness. Bronze statue by J H Foley, erected in 1875 in the precincts of St Patrick's Cathedral, Dublin.
5. St Stephen's Green, Dublin, c.1895, from the Lawrence Collection. By courtesy of the National Gallery.
6. The second Earl of Iveagh. A copy of the portrait in oils by H A Olivier.
7. Bishop Clayton's house: a reconstruction of the façade erected in 1736 to the designs of Richard Castle. Drawn by Nicholas Sheaff.
8. Iveagh House, the entrance front. A modern view of the façade erected in 1866 to the designs of Sir Benjamin Lee Guinness.
9,10. Ground-floor plan and first-floor plan of Iveagh House. Measured and drawn by Nicholas Sheaff.
11. The entrance hall, with the inner hall beyond.
12. Wooden bas-relief panel in the entrance hall: *Priam entreats Achilles to release the body of Hector.*
13. Wooden bas-relief panel in the entrance hall: *Achilles plays his lyre.*
14. *The Shepherd Boy.* Sculpture in white marble by John Hogan, 1846.
15. Carved wooden chimney-piece in the inner hall.
16. *The reading Girl.* Sculpture in white marble by Pietro Magni, mid-19th century.
17. The old dining-room.
18. Detail of ornamental plaster frieze in the old dining-room.
19. Door-case in the ante-room.
20. Detail of carved wooden frieze of the old dining-room chimney-piece.
21. The stairhall with the ballroom vestibule beyond, seen from the first-floor landing.
22. The stairhall ceiling.
23. The ground-floor curtail of the staircase.
24. Central wrought-iron panel of the staircase landing.
25. Detail of the carved wooden frontispiece to the staircase landing.
26. The old music-room.
27. Detail of the ceiling plasterwork of the old music-room.
28. Brass door furniture in the old music-room.
29. *The ruins of the Forum at Rome.* Oil on canvas by George Barret.
30. *View of Tivoli and the Temple of Vesta.* Oil on canvas by George Barret.
31. *The ruins of the Coliseum.* Oil on canvas by George Barret.
32. Chimney-piece in the old music-room.
33. Detail of ornamental plaster frieze in the old music-room
34. Door-case in the old music-room.
35. The saloon.
36. The saloon ceiling.
37. The drawing-room.
38. Chimney-piece in the drawing-room.
39. Door-case in the drawing-room.
40. Oak panelling and door-case in the old library.
41. Carved wooden chimney-piece in the old library.
42. The Adam room.
43. The ballroom.
44. Chimney-piece and ornamental plasterwork in the ballroom.
45. An end bay in the ballroom.
46. Stone pavilion in the garden of Iveagh House.

References

THE EIGHTEENTH-CENTURY HOUSE

The setting: St Stephen's Green
1. John T Gilbert, ed., *Calendar of Ancient Records of Dublin*, vol. IV., Dublin, 1894, p 298.
2. F Elrington Ball, ed., *The Correspondence of Jonathan Swift*, vol. I, London, 1910, p 128.
3. James Malton, *A Picturesque and Descriptive View of the City of Dublin*, London, 1792-9.
4. *Universal Magazine*, 3 January 1749.
5. I am paraphrasing here Walter Harris, *The History and Antiquities of the City of Dublin*, Dublin and London, 1766, Appendix, section XV, p 481.
6. Eleanor Butler, 'The Georgian Squares of Dublin, part I', *Country Life*, vol. 100, p 758.
7. Walter Harris, op. cit., p 481, note (a).

The patron: Bishop Clayton
1. Elizabeth Thomson, the editress of *Memoirs of Viscountess Sundon, Mistress of the Robes to Queen Caroline, Consort of George II*, London, 1847, vol. II, p 4.
2. Thomson, op. cit., vol. I, p 27.
3. Thomson, op. cit., vol. II, p 25.
4. Lady Llanover, ed., *The Autobiography and Correspondence of Mary Granville, Mrs Delany*, London 1861, vol. I, p 287.
5. This is the only conclusion I can offer after an exhaustive search in the Registry of Deeds, Dublin. The house, which is described in Llanover, loc. cit., cannot be located elsewhere on St Stephen's Green, nor on any of the streets leading to the square. But the conclusion cannot, at present, be corroborated as the book of abstracts dealing with York Street leases in this period has been missing for some years from the Registry of Deeds.
6. Llanover, op. cit., vol. I, p 354.
7. Ibid., p 372.
8. Countess of Cork and Orrery, ed., *The Orrery Papers*, London, 1903, vol. I, p 206.
9. Orrery is here paraphrasing Alexander Pope, *Epistle to Lord Burlington of the Use of Riches*, line 36.
10. Orrery, op. cit., vol. I, p 177.
11. Llanover, op. cit., vol. II, p 394.
12. Ibid., p 489.
13. Registry of Deeds, Dublin, Lib. 295, p 161, No. 195382, *Roberts Solrs to Bishop of Clogher*.
14. Llanover, op. cit., vol. II, p 399.
15. *An Essay on Spirit, wherein the Doctrine of the Trinity is considered in the Light of Nature and Reason; as well as in the Light in which it was held by the ancient Hebrews: compared also with the Doctrine of the Old and New Testament. With an Enquiry into the Sentiments of the Primitive Fathers of the Church; and The Doctrine of the Trinity as maintained by the Egyptians, Pythagoreans, and Platonists. Together with some Remarks on the Athanasian and Nicene Creeds.* Dublin, 1751.
16. A full list of Clayton's works can be found in W Maziere Brady, DD, *Clerical and Parochial Records of Cork, Cloyne and Ross*, Dublin, 1864, vol. III, pp 76-8.
17. See *Robert Clayton, Bishop of Clogher, A Vicar of the Church of Ireland, Bishop Clayton on the Nicene and Athanasian Creeds. Republished with a Memoir*, 1876, (copy at Royal Irish Academy).
18. Orrery, op. cit., vol. II, p 135.

The architect: Richard Castle
1. Registry of Deeds, Dublin, Lib. 82, p 486, no. 58697, *Russell to Bp. of Cork and Ross*.
2. King's Hospital Archives, *Rent ledger, 1730-46*; ground rent payments began on 29 September 1736, 9/2d per annum.
3. The Knight of Glin, 'Richard Castle, Architect. His biography and works, a synopsis', *Quarterly Bulletin of the Irish Georgian Society*, January-March 1964, p 32. I have drawn largely on the Knight of Glin's excellent account for facts and dates concerning Castle's work.
4. Richard Boyle, third Earl of Burlington and fourth Earl of Cork (1694-1753), the doyen of British Palladian circles.
5. Orrery, op. cit., vol. I, p 177.
6. See 'Richard Castles', *Anthologia Hibernica*, vol. II, October 1793.
7. In reconstructing the façade, I have relied on the following: plan of the house in John Rocque, *An Exact Survey of the City and Suburbs of Dublin*, Dublin, 1756; distant views of the house in James Malton, op. cit., engraving, and James Mahony, *View of Dublin 1853*, National Gallery of Ireland; and written description in *Georgian Society Records*, Dublin, 1910, vol. II, p 83.
8. A scheme of 1740 by Castle for a new dining hall at Trinity College uses Jones's Tuscan order and eaves pediment in a very literal manner (Elevation, TCD Mss).
9. *Dublin Chronicle*, 22 January 1788, p 290, and *Anthologia Hibernica* loc. cit.

Later owners
1. Llanover, op. cit., vol. III, p 493.
2. *Georgian Society Records*, vol. II, p 83.
3. Maurice Craig, *Dublin 1660-1860*, London, 1952, pp 275-7 et passim
4. Registry of Deeds, Dublin, Lib. 668, p 516, no. 466082.
5. Registry of Deeds, Dublin, Lib. 744, p 475, no. 506810, and p 476, no. 506811.
6. Registry of Deeds, Dublin, 1856, bk 13, no. 9.

THE NINETEENTH-CENTURY HOUSE

The Guinness family
1. In writing this brief account of the Guinness family and the Guinness brewery, I have drawn largely on Patrick Lynch and John Vaizey, *Guinness's Brewery in the Irish Economy, 1759-1876*, Cambridge, 1960.
2. *The Dublin Builder*, vol. V; 1863, p 183.

3. Quoted in P Lynch and J Vaizey, op. cit., p 181.
4. See especially *The Dublin Builder*, vol. V, 1863, p 5.
5. *The Irish Builder*, vol. X, 1868, p 99.
6. P Lynch and J Vaizey, op. cit., p 260.
7. Ibid., p 193.
8. Ibid., p 194
9. *The Irish Builder*, vol. XII, 1870, p 133.
10. Letters to *The Irish Builder*, vol. XIV, 1872, p 147.
11. *Dictionary of National Biography, 1922-30*, London, 1930, article by A. Cochrane.
12. P Lynch and J Vaizey, op. cit., p 189.
13. Llanover, op. cit., vol. I, p 295.

The creation of the modern Iveagh House
1. Registry of Deeds, Dublin, 1862, bk 29, no. 10.
2. *The Dublin Builder*, vol. VIII, 1866, p 29.
3. *Patterson, Kempster, and Shortall Records* (at the National Trust Archive, Dublin), bills of quantity, bks 10 and 11.
4. *Patterson, Kempster and Shortall Records*, completion of staircase; bills of quantity, bk 11, p 11-31.
5. *Patterson, Kempster, and Shortall Records*, bills of quantity, bk 12, pp 318-57.
6. *Patterson, Kempster and Shortall Records*, bills of quantity, bk 10, p 517.
7. Battersby & Co., *No. 80 St Stephen's Green, Dublin,* Sale Catalogue, Dublin 1939.
8. *Patterson, Kempster and Shortall Records*, bills of quantity, bk 6, pp 525-530.
9. Ibid., p 64.
10. Ibid., pp 359-389; and bk 7, pp 185-203.
11. *Patterson, Kempster and Shortall Records*, bills of quantity, bk 7, pp 1-6, 32-40, 312-323.
12. *The Irish Builder*, vol. XLII, 1900, p 346.

The remodelling of St Stephen's Green
1. Gilbert, op. cit., vol. XIV, p 275.
2. Gilbert, op. cit., vol. XVI, p 185.
3. *The Irish Builder*, vol. XX, 1878, p 81.
4. *The Dublin Builder*, vol. V, 1863, p 171.
5. Samuel A Ossory Fitzpatrick, *Dublin; A Historical and Topographical Account of the City*, London, 1907, p 197.
6. *The Irish Builder*, vol. XXXVI, 1894, p 137.
7. *Patterson, Kempster and Shortall Records*, ledger bk 1872-82, p 268.
8. A watercolour perspective of the design is preserved at the Sir Hugh Lane Municipal Gallery, Dublin.

DESCRIPTION OF THE HOUSE
1. Henry Parkinson and Peter Lund Simmonds, *The Illustrated Record and descriptive catalogue of the Dublin International Exhibition of 1865*, London, 1866, p 474; *The Letter*, No. 41; *Joy*, No. 13; *Modesty*, No. 42; *Sleeping Faun and Satyr*, no. 15.
2. *Iliad*, bk XXIV. The early eighteenth century saw an upsurge of interest in Homer's classic work. A French translation by Mme Dacier appeared in 1711, with illustrations by Bernard Picart, and this was rendered into English by John Ozell in 1712. Alexander Pope's new English translation was published 1715-20. But of particular relevance to these carved panels is the appearance of *Homeri Ilias*, vol. I, 1729, vol. II, 1732, a Greek and Latin version by Dr Clayton's theological mentor, Dr Samuel Clarke.
3. *Iliad*, bk IX.
4. H Parkinson and P L Simmonds op. cit., *Modesty*, no. 13.
5. William Kent, *The Designs of Inigo Jones ...*, London, 1727, 1st vol., plate 64.
6. The surround is different in style from those in the 1866 rooms, but similar to neo-Palladian examples at St Anne's, Clontarf.
7. H Parkinson and P L Simmonds, op. cit., *The reading Girl*, No. 16.
8. Now in Alte Pinakothek, Munich.
9. *Patterson, Kempster and Shortall Records*, bills of quantity, bk 9, pp 905-13, and bk 11, pp 1-31.
10. C P Curran, in *Dublin decorative Plasterwork*, London, 1967, p 23, dates the ceiling to "about 1730". This would pre-date the erection of the house itself and is clearly incorrect
11. Sebastiano Serlio, *Five Books of Architecture*, bk 3.
12. *Georgian Society Records*, vol. II, 1910, p 84, and plates LXXXII and LXXXIII. The mistake was corrected in vol. III, p xxvi.
13. See Eileen Harris, *The Furniture of Robert Adam*, London, 1973, chapter IV.
14. *The Irish Builder*, vol. XLII, 1900, p 346.
15. *The Irish Builder*, vol. XLVIII, 1906, p 142, letter from John Ryan.
16. *The Irish Builder*, vol. XLII, 1900, p 346.
17. Ibid.

IVEAGH GARDENS

1. Maurice Craig, op. cit., pp 226-9.
2. 'Lawn' was a term used in Ireland as a general description of a grassy landscape foreground to a large house.
3. See plan 122, and plan 469 (2), *Wide Streets Commission maps*, Public Record Office, Dublin.
4. *The Dublin Builder*, vol. V, 1863, p 178.
5. Registry of Deeds, Dublin, 1862, bk 13, no. 250.
6. *The Dublin Builder*, vol. V, 1863, p 71.
7. Ibid., p 178.
8. Ibid., p 71.
9. Registry of Deeds, Dublin, 1870, bk 24, no. 250.

Index

Adam style, 19th-century revival of, 49
Ardilaun, 1st Lord, see Guinness, Sir Arthur Edward
Ashford Castle, Co. Galway, 20, 21

Ballyhaise, Co. Cavan, 16
Barret, George (painter), 42
Barry, Dr Edward, 15
Bernini, Gianlorenzo (sculptor), 37
Bolingbroke, Henry St John, 1st Vct., 14
Boschi, Giuseppe (sculptor), 51
Brooking, Charles (cartographer), 11
Burlington, Richard, 3rd Earl of, 16
Burton, Charles, 17, 57
Butler, Rudolph Maximilian (architect), 55

Caroline, Queen of Great Britain and Ireland, 13
Carton, Co. Kildare, 45
Castle, Richard (architect), 11, 14, 16-17, 21, 27, 31, 33, 34, 37, 45, 57, 61 *The architect* (note 8)
— his Tuscan portico to Bishop Clayton's house, 17
— his use of mahogany, 40, 45
Celtic revival in architecture, 55
Clarke, Dr Samuel, 13, 62 *Description* (note 2)
Clayton, Mrs, Mistress of the Robes, 13, 14
Clayton, Mrs Catherine, 13-15, 17, 57
Clayton, Rev. John, 13
Clayton, Dr Robert, 11, 13-15, 16, 17, 19, 23, 33, 40, 45, 54, 57, 62 *Description* (note 2)
Clogher, Bishopric of, 14
Clonmel, Jack Scott, 1st Earl of, 54
— Thomas, 2nd Earl of, 54
— John Henry, 3rd Earl of, 54
Commissioners of Encumbered Estates 17, 18, 57
Commissioners of Public Works in Ireland, 23, 55
Commissioners of Wide Streets, 54
Cooke, W H Howard (architect), 25
Corbellini, Quintilio (sculptor), 33
Corelli, Arcangelo, 14
Cork & Ross, Bishopric of, 14
Cousins, A L (civil engineer), 23
Curran, Rt. Hon. John Philpot, 17, 57
Curran, Sarah, 17

The Daily Express, 19
Darcy Bros., (builders and stuccodores), 51
Dargan, William, 19
Delany, Mrs Mary, 11, 13, 14, 20, 31
Department of Foreign (previously External) Affairs, 25, 57
de Valera, Eamon, 25
Dingley, Mrs Rebecca, 11
Donnellan, Catherine, see Clayton, Mrs Catherine

Drew, Sir Thomas (architect), 21
Dublin, Aldborough House, 27
Bective House, 17
City Assembly, 11
Clonmel House, 54
Clonmel Street, 54
Coburg Gardens, 19, 54
Coombe Lying-in Hospital, 20
Custom House, 51
Harcourt Street, 54
Nos 9 and 10, Henrietta Street, 17
House of Lords, 15
Hugh Lane Municipal Gallery of Modern Art, 24
Iveagh House, bachelors' wing, 21, 25
            — 18th-century sculpture at, 31, 33, 34, 37, 48, 49
            — gift of to the Irish nation, 25
            — neo-Georgian design at, 21, 27, 31, 33, 34, 37, 45, 47 48, 49, 51
            — ornamental metalwork at, 27, 37, 51
            — ornamental plasterwork at, 17, 34, 37, 40, 45, 47, 48, 49, 51, 62 *Description* (note 10)
Leeson's Fields, 54
No. 18, Leeson Street Lower, 21
Leinster House, 16, 17, 40
Mountcashel House, 17
Parliament House, 16
Royal University, 55
St Patrick's Cathedral restoration, 19, 21, 23
St Stephen's Green, 11-12, 13, 16, 17, 19, 54
            — Commissioners of, 23
            — Firework display of 1749, 11
            — proposed mansion house for Corporation, 23
            — monument to George II, 11, 23, 24
            — monument proposed to Duke of Wellington, 23
            — Nos. 78 and 79, 21, 27, 37, 49, 57
            — No. 81, 21, 57
            — No. 85, 11, 17, 33, 37, 45
            — Nos. 119-120, 11
            — remodelling of 1877-80, 20, 23-24
Thomas Street, 19
Trinity College, 13
            — Provost's house, 37, 47
Tyrone House, 17, 40
University College, 55
York Street, 13, 61 *The Patron* (note 5)
The Dublin (later Irish) Builder 23, 51
Dublin Exhibition of 1865, 19, 31, 54
— of 1872, 20, 55
Dublin Exhibition Palace and Winter Garden Company, 19, 20, 54-55

Elveden Hall, Suffolk, 20, 21

63

Emmet, Robert, 17
An Essay on Spirit, 14, 15
A Defence of the Essay on Spirit, 14

Farmleigh, Co. Dublin, 20, 21, 25
Farrell, Sir Thomas (sculptor), 23
Foley, J H (sculptor), 19
Francini Brothers, (stuccodores), 45
Fuller, J F (architect), 21, 23, 27, 33, 34, 37, 40, 48, 49

The Georgian Society Records 47, 61   *The architect*
Gillows of Lancaster, (furnishers), 49
Gladstone, William Ewart, 19
Grand Canal of Ireland, 23
The 'Grand Tour,' 13
Guinness, Arthur, 19
  — Arthur, Son and Co., 19, 20
  — Sir Arthur Edward, 20, 21, 23
  —·Sir Benjamin Lee, 18, 19-20, 21, 23, 27, 31, 33, 34, 47, 48, 54, 55, 57
  — Edward Cecil, 20, 21, 25, 49, 51, 55, 57
  — Rupert Edward Cecil, 25, 55, 57

Hadfield, M E (architect), 21
Harris, Walter (historian), 11
Hazlewood, Co. Sligo, 16
Hogan, John (sculptor), 33-34
Holkham Hall, Norfolk, 51
Horace, (Latin poet), 15
Hosmer, Harriet (sculptress), 31
Houghton, John (sculptor), 31
Houghton Hall, Norfolk, 33, 51
Hume, David, 14

The Iliad, 31, 33, 48, 62 *Description* (note 2)
Inisfallen, Co. Kerry, oratory, 55
Iveagh, 1st Earl of, see Guinness, Edward Cecil
— 2nd Earl of, see Guinness, Rupert
Iveagh Trust, 20

Jones, Alfred G (architect), 19
Jones, Inigo (architect), 17, 61 *The architect* (note 8)

Kent, William (architect), 33, 45
Killala, Bishopric of, 13, 14

Latham, James (painter), 14
Leinster, Duke of, 19
Lombardi, G B (sculptor), 31
London, No. 44 Berkeley Square, 45
No. 5 Berkeley Street, 20
Devonshire House, Piccadilly, 13
Hampton Court, 54
The Mall, 11
St James's, Westminster, 13
St Paul's, Covent Garden, 17
War Office, Whitehall, 21
Lutyens, Sir Edwin (architect), 24

Magni, Pietro (sculptor), 34
Mahony, James (painter), 61 *The architect* (note 7)
Malton, James (writer and engraver), 11, 24, 61 *The architect* (note 7)
Maratta, Carlo (painter),14
Marlborough, Sarah, 1st Duchess of, 13
May, Hugh (architect), 13
McCarthy, J J (architect), 19
McGrath, Raymond (architect), 25, 47, 51
McMahon, Rt Hon. Sir William, 17, 57
Moore, Christopher (sculptor), 34
Morat, Carlo, see Maratta, Carlo
Morrison of Edinburgh (furnishers)**,** 51
Mountcashel, 1st Countess, 17, 57
— Stephen, 2nd Viscount and 1st Earl of, 17, 34, 57
— Stephen, 2nd Earl of, 17, 57

Newman, John Henry, Cardinal, 55
Niven, Ninian (landscape architect), 54

Orrery, John 5th Earl of, 14, 16, 45

Pater, Jean-Baptiste (painter), 47
Pearce, Sir Edward Lovett (architect), 16, 17
Pendarves, Mrs Mary; see Delany, Mrs Mary
Penn, William, 14
Pope, Alexander, 61 *The patron* (note 9), 62 *Description* (note 2)

Roberts, S N (architect), 21
Rocque, John (cartographer), 61 *The architect* (note 7)
Rome, Temple of Bacchus, 45
Rubens, Sir Peter Paul (painter), 34
Russborough, Co. Wicklow, 40

St Anne's, Co. Dublin, 20, 21, 34, 62 *Description* (note 6)
St Wolstan's, Co. Kildare, 14
Serlio, Sebastiano (architect), 45
Shaw, Richard Norman (architect), 51
Sibthorpe & Son , (Furnishers and Decorators) , 49
Sinai, hieroglyphics in, 14
'Stella', (Mrs Esther Johnson), 11
Sundon, 1st Viscountess, see Clayton, Mrs, Mistress of the Robes
Swift, Dr Jonathan, 11

Tantardini, Antonio (sculptor), 31
Thorwaldsen, Bertel (sculptor), 33
Tijou, Jean (ironsmith), 51
Trinity, doctrine of the 13, 14
Tuam, Archbishopric of, 14

The United Irishmen, 17

Van Nost, John (sculptor), 11, 23
Versailles, palace of, 51
Vitruvius Pollio (ancient Roman architect), 14

Wales, Edward, Prince of, 19
Walpole, Sir Robert, 13
Waterhouse, Alfred (architect), 21
Watteau, Jean-Antoine (Painter), 47
West, Mrs Elisa, 18
West, Robert Beatty, 17, 57

Young, William (architect), 21, 37, 49, 51